the silent poems

Tabor Sarah Books   Oakland : Palo Alto

the
silent
poems

TEYA SCHAFFER

Layout: Spitfire Graphics
Illustration: Susan Liroff

Publisher's Cataloging-in-Publication Data

Schaffer, Teya
  The Silent Poems
Teya Schaffer — 1st ed.

  I. Title
811.54
ISBN 9780-935079210

CONTENTS

A a a b C D c e f g i J j d L j m l k z o m Q q r s t

Invitation to a Reader

Without you the I
lonely as evidence after a trial, and morose
an ashtray collecting dust
—forget this I, obviously
someone is waving a flask of intention.

Your eyes may have forgotten this motion.
Perhaps it was death licked your lids
to a closing or your glance may be too lively
hurrying towards conclusion and a thought
to rest on.

Let me introduce an image
sincere and awkward as a kneeling
camel: My lifeline is end-stopped
and subtle as a desert for lack of you.
When entering these words
bring water.

WAKING

How Memory Returns

You are
facing the bathroom sink, toothbrush in hand,
when a half-phrase in an unknown language
perhaps Bulgarian
falls off your bewildered lips.
Continues to fall. An avalanche of the unintelligible.
You attempt something simple—your name,
but it resists translation.
The tiled walls appear not to have changed.
It probably is not safe to go out in this condition.
If you concentrate
the false starts of your breath will calm.
There is no reason to believe
syllables have come from behind an iron curtain,
refugees crossing your throat on an icy track,
though they sway
and jostle their neighbors. Everyone on board
seems suspicious and uneasy. You think,
"This must be the winter of 19—"
but you are only imagining a national hunger,
an excuse for shivering as the sounds approach sentences.
The windows flash light: border crossings, Sofia,

then go dark with reflections: passengers, the tiled interior
of a small compartment; light; dark; a chill
if his hand had made a sound—this cannot go on
forever—the toothbrush becomes a needle
stitching your lips closed.
Besides it is not Bulgarian after all,
but a code from a hidden year
in your own life. You are free to go now.
You leave quickly, believing your quiet can be trusted.
You leave thoroughly, the tongue of the door locked in its frame.
Even so, there is a shadow across your day, and at night
your dreams parse *it is as if, it is as if.*

RED RIDING

You look back and sure enough
all the breadcrumbs have been eaten by birds.
The trees collude, darkening the path
the handkerchief with its red drops of warning
the glass mountain, the nettle sweaters.
The end of *once upon a time* is coming closer,
worlds returning to words, words to sounds,
the alphabet an open jaw with 26 sharp teeth.

THE NARRATIVE WILL OUT

1
The triangle A and its small apple.
A thick pencil scoring coarse-grained paper.

The transition from words to worlds
a book where houses walk on chicken legs
magic in the horse's head, the virgin's mouth
silence a sister stitching nettles.
Beauty sleeps in a tower
riddles rhyme.

Four sisters in *Little Women* and in the family.
Go Fish, Old Maid, and the flip-flap of War.
Above our hands, the play of words:
nursery rhymes and knock-knock jokes
imagining what lay beyond the rooftops of heaven
considerations of value: an arm, a leg.
Silence too: staring contests, breath-holding contests
the longest-sound-one-exhalation-can-carry
contests. Cries of victory and accusation.
Wrestling: knees and elbows.
Fighting: fingernails and teeth.

On the sidewalk, we smack wrapped bars
of Bonomo's Turkish Taffy.

Early knowledge: the alphabet must be shattered
before it can speak.

2
Want travels an open road: *lack* and *desire*.
Everything hidden wants discovery.

"What's done is done." Our mother's motto
pushed us over every day's past.
"The atom bomb could fall by then"
swept the future. In between
the rise of afternoons held by the nape.
Her hands lifting us by those thin sticks
our arms, the escape from gravity's pull
into hers, eyes wide to the furniture,
flight and landing.

3
The maple tree and books.
A college sanctuary.
People. Life.

4
I buy my son a punching bag.
It hangs like a torso on a thick link chain.

My father begins dying; he should leave faster.
I pray to every sky: don't make me visit.

Three ways of hitting,
one easy kick, thigh thumping
against canvas,
gloved fists and elbows.
I think I know their faces.
I think I know the history of my face.
Why then this panic?

The airline workers call a strike.
The bag hangs like a torso
or a dream
wanting interpretation.

5
Hold the canvas steady
in both hands.
Stand on one leg.
Bend the other knee.
I was not there for my awakening
so you must imagine your thigh
lifting to bump against
a heavy sand-filled bag
which hangs like a torso.
Imagine the thump of contact.
The bag tries to sway away.
Remember to hold it.
Remember to switch legs.
Keep going.

Don't forget to be angry.
When the words spring
like a trap
don't listen.

6
Seated at my desk, I discover myself
sitting there. Cut threads of thought.
Small moments of amnesia.

The house had never felt the need to talk to me before,
it has to raise its voice to be heard.
Get out! Get out!
No smoke. No intruder.
The walls—all the walls—in sudden concussive
choirs of alarm *Go! Flee!*
Nonsense, I argue. There's nothing wrong,
I protest, gathering wallet, book, pen.
Running.

Usually to the marina. Wind and water.
Sometimes just to the car. Where I sit
staring at the foolish house.

I can do the math: one talking house, one dying father,
one daughter whose running shoes erase the answer.

Sometimes days pass without disturbance.
Without disturbance of that nature. But I am disturbed.

Not all of it is interesting. There are pathetic elements:
the bleating, the thin voice of need.
Sometimes I fold like a straw wrapper
twisting in nervous hands.

7
If you don't know something is missing
when do you look for it?
And if it came looking for you
a hot breath against the cheek
a stubble of crude graffiti
with what pen would you
write it?

GEOGRAPHY

*Joseph named the first-born Manasseh, meaning
"God has made me forget completely my hardship
and my parental home."* Genesis 41.51

Canaan was a hesitation in his mouth,
the Jordan pulsed softly beneath his left eye.
I was the cloak of my father's amnesia,
his fingers frayed the border.

WAKING

The past is a dry grave, its bones twice-turned and breaking
I sleep on its apron

A memory twists my dreams
I fold it flat as forgetting in a book of nightmare

He had no right to die with his mouth open
His restless stammer waking my ear

A small man's death pours night through day
Dreams sift through speech, amnesia's concordance

Later I'll find the books that make this real
Now my house shrills *not fire, not intruder, not safe*

Witnesses claim Rumpelstiltskin stomped the earth and it
   swallowed
First one angry leg, then the other   Someone knew his name

The one who spun in the dark unraveling his face
Now semaphores through daylight with a dead body: *All
   vows revoked*

My father has rescinded our silence
The nightmare assailants fade away, replaced

Ask me: I prefer the story of strange men stalking my sleep
Tell me: what becomes of the changeling after the tale is told.

VALENTINE

One sister bought our parents
as an anniversary gift
tickets to a Broadway show,
while buying herself,
a teenager
running away
to sunny California,
time to taxi to the airport.

I was less clever.
I left and left.
Once
our parents
had my friends
arrested
for the theft
of a jewel,
which was
actually me
headed for
that same
airport.

Finally
I crept away
under the cover of letters
with false postmarks.

Today I give these stories
as an excuse
a brag
a valentine
to seal new friendships:
imagine the snows I shoveled
to get to you.

THE TIME I TRY TO LEAVE HOME FOR CALIFORNIA

that day two of my sisters know what is coming and split
before I make for the door with Peter and Vince, summer
of love, and my father there before us, hand on the lock,
shouting he'll call the cops, say they've stolen the jewels, and
mother yelling "She doesn't have a penis, she can't go," and
none of us able to laugh, only very nervous smiles, and then
the boys are kicked out and I wild sprint after, the youngest
siblings caught inside with their noses up against the door
glass as sun sets on the neighbors' with a cop car and my
parents pressing charges and neighbor saying if he had a
hairbrush and I were his daughter; and for weeks after I can
only leave the house if my little brother's attached and I take
Janie to the principal's saying my sister's in your school and
there's trouble in our home and he says if I had a hairbrush
and you were my daughter; that was the time my parents
told my sister they'd keep her locked up if I ran away and
she told me *run.*

On Seeing My Mother

One of us was supposed to mellow with age
taking lessons from the body
which ripens and falls.
Our breasts follow gravity
and our bellies
rise to meet them.
Her admonition
to stand tall
is silenced
by small erosions
but our teeth
still grind the past
and hold everything
back. Here, on the steep slope
to her husband's grave,
my mother hesitates.
Lifts her foot
and cannot set it
forward.
I slip behind her
like the shadow
of her coat
arms beneath arms
belly to back,

walking her uphill
like the kindly daughter
of an elderly parent.
She imagines herself
a woman of open arms
embraced.
"You go first,"
I tell her
meaning all of it:
forgiveness
and death.

LUCID FOR THE DOCTOR

Our elderly mother rediscovers
the connection of dots
whenever a doctor appears.
Lucid has never been less clear
how does the food come from?
why don't I know? wheeled
from corner to corner
I don't know the plan
retirement home to clinic where
suddenly
the place she lives
becomes the place she lives
and it is we
excitable, demanding, unreliable
children
who must be confused.
Our mother isn't—
and she never—
not now, not then.

MATERNAL FRACTURES

Another thing that passes for funny in our family: the
surgeon pointing to the waiting room, "Of course you'll
want to be there." Sister plans to find three new fulltime
jobs. I flaunt a jury summons. Brother's already done
the lion's share. In case what goes around doesn't actually
return, we push hard on the wheel.

SORORITY

Over the telephone line, we console each other
for our mother's continued health.

Poor woman, no worse than many, better than some,
now so brain-fuddled she uses please and thank you.

Our hunger snakes through the conversation:
"She's frail but going strong." "Damn it."

Usually we'd laugh but this time a silence
which deepens into dark water

we are honoring the oaths made while drowning.
Our own children's hair: barely damp.

Water Closes the Mouth

The child
drops beneath the shimmering surface
slowly
quietly
face tilting upward
arms floating
no flutter
no kick
a cherub
probably
has no use
for breath
one plump leg
slightly bent
as if sinking
he climbed

he falls
without panic
without flailing
in pure faith of retrieval
though water
replaces
the space
he held
and all around me
water thick as glass
the chlorine rising
the distance between us
immeasurable
and increasing

FLOATERS

The eye's vitreous gel
detaches the retinal tissue
with a delicate tug
as if opening a gift
wrapped by the irreplaceable child
to whom it might matter
that you create a separation
slowly
smiling
as between sticky tape
and glitter wrap
you insert a torn fingernail's edge.

The gift slides out
like this:
    black threads
    ink in water, twigs
    flowing from a nib
    on wet paper.
They float between light and retina
without harming the apple of your eye.

LOVE, OH

1985

The assimilation of a shocking experience
how is it done? Even the flood
of loving, my heart
exquisitely aware
kind
and caring,
is a shock requiring notice
and recuperation.

LOVE, OH CARELESS

When I consider the care
the timing, the risk
when I told her
birds in the air   stars in the sky
and she bravely translated *Are you saying*
—she sighed the word itself—*love?*
oh love
right there above the vegetable tempura
and I *yes* ducked under the table
and she *me too* tossed a napkin over her face.
We knew what we entered; we gave love its due.

That was 20 years ago. Since then time's been busy
laying the dust of everything on everything.
And some of that is the dust of the dead
which is to say she died, and time kept busy.
Now I say *Love! Love!* as one says salt
sprinkling its one round syllable
on every available surface: a good joke
a book of poems, my students
who warily note their teacher's hunger
for words. Today's lesson is fragments:
Birds in the air. Stars in the sky.

WORRY IS LIKE A PRAYER PERFORMED

Jolted awake by the Big One
steel-toed boots might fill with glass
sneakers take cover under bed.
Even now the ceiling fingers its cracks.
I shove a reluctant flashlight
firmly under mattress
while reciting the locations
of water bottles and family.
It is 1989; the Bay Bridge has come down;
you are still alive, but I can see my future
on the cherry wood dresser: coins and keys
preparing to drift with the continent.

REHEARSAL

Beneath your skin
more mystery
than I desire
the living pulse
struggling through
a narrowed aorta
knotted cells
clinging to
esophagus
my place
in the viewing
stands—
you raise your skeleton
to the sun, bone scan
hot spots *femur*
vertebra skull.
I look through you.

I look at you.

Later, sex
that little mouse
of malleable bones
the quiver of alertness
which announces your
presence
its insistence on love
inseparable
from body—why
and for what
good purpose?

My cries end in tears.
Yours in sleep.

THE HOMEFRONT *for Richie*

Because we leave home with our genders on
when I write us, *we are nameless.*

I scrape butter across the toast
you scoop bread through yogurt.
In the newspaper, other rhythms.
It is 2002. We are going to war.
We are resisting the war.
Everything is worse than it has been:
police and soldiers
lives wrenched apart
the inevitable pleasure
as we commiserate
before entering
our separate days.

I bring five senses of imagination to war;
they stop at the brink: the meaning of acrid
when placed next to gun.
Your childhood also eludes me: the mother
whose lullabies predicted her early death,
the city which kept tumbling down,
how the hearthstone came into your keeping.

35 years beneath a shingled roof.
You kept the child fed and the house
in place when my spouse was dying.
If friend were a larger word than family
it would suffice.

Her lamp remains. Every day
it grants the same wish.

Be my history. Survive me.

CEMETERY VISITS

The grass has pulled all the rain inside itself
and given back dainty yellow flowers.
The baby has two new pinwheels.
An orange balances on polished brass and
a border of bricks confirms a marriage.
At the turn of the road, her stone's comment:
not lost but dead.
I touch the grass in case it remembers,
as a mattress does, the body which shaped it.

AN EDUCATED GRIEF

On the blackboard, a white chalk horizon.

Length can be a grammar of time
an x of now, short slashes of then

or an arithmetic problem
with zero hung between plus and minus.

Thus in history class, you become
the past

while in math, you remain a possibility
even when canceled.

BIRDFEEDER

Our neighbor has evidence: what grows between us
is intolerable—a shrub, she says.
It blooms like a cloud, spreads like exaggeration,
is generous as love leaning towards home—
can I say it more clearly?
squirrels play "hamsters in a cage"
roof, tree, roof, fence, roof, tree
circling the yard, all squeak and natter.
Birds are deep in the green.

Our neighbor believes untidy plants belong in the wild,
that the hedge is unwieldy, that the tree is,
quite simply, a shrub.
It sheds white petals all summer long;
they brown on ivy and old paint cans,
camouflage the containers equipped for disaster
—water, radio, the old eyeglasses yellowing
with the relief of disuse. The tree
oblivious, careless, extends branch and shadow
into the heat. I drift below, dreaming resurrections:
a bird in the nest of my lover.

Our neighbor believes in a perfectable universe,
an Eden of uprooting. My grief outwits her.
It is the summer of a friend's dying: there are things
I will not hear of, and unheard remains undone.
The next year, I stall with Solomonic compromise:
half the tree is mine to save. She is unimpressed.
Then the Trade Center falls, making her enmity
poor form.

Our neighbor was a forest ranger but she lives
in the city. In the third year, I recognize my failures
and take pictures: the tree in a window frame,
the tree as a very blue sky embellished by green.
It joins the other lives flattened in my album,
the lover, the friend, the—was it really a shrub?
In her yard, a green wire cage rises on a metal pole.
The birds go there to eat.

WHAT ENTITLES US

to pleasure,
the sun-warmed
automobile,
its four syllables of self-
propulsion?
By good fortune:
nothing.
Luck falls
witless
as dandelion seed,
blown by wind
camouflaged
in fur.

My Son's Cat Grown Old

My son grew old enough to leave a cat
to his mother's care; a careless thing,
though he loves us both, because I do not
love cats. She takes me, mistakenly,
for a surrogate. Calls me by my son's name
Meow which means "mine." From room
to room, she whines her want of attention
then sits by the food dish as if expecting a feast.
Desperate or bored, she throws herself into the traffic
of my feet. I wouldn't mind kicking her.
Instead I trip.
I stumble.
I have to get down on my knees
saying *kitty kitty are you hurt* when it is all her own fault.
All day I hiss *get* and *go 'way* lifting her off of me.
She is insistent as a toddler. And old, as cats go.
Dozes, naps, sleeps; measures the leap and turns
back as if indifferent. She stares at the backdoor
remembering —and bends me to her will:
Cat, I curse, *you'll be the death of me* for she will not
go out unless she can escape back in and I
cannot watch forever against what would enter
an open door. But she must be allowed
animal odors and forsythia. I stand guard, then slip
deep into the house where I forget to worry.
I go as far away as memory, the door wide open
cat at my feet.

ECCLESIASTES

THEOLOGY

The Jews were not promised eternal life therefore
the rabbis do not practice abstinence and my arms
lift the light weight of the hugest words.
Their meanings are tucked into Greek
like a child to bed: *eros thanatos.*

SANDY, EVER AFTER

I am thinking of a blue bowl
an earth blue, possibly cobalt
a color not seen in the sky.
And this blue bowl
has a presence   most often
in the kitchen dish rack
next to the white bowl
(we've only the two
for cereal), and next often
in my thought   when I decide
white or blue, bowl or her.
It all happens that quickly,
bowl or presence
bowl or absence.
When I observe it: lustrous,
an inch of concentric circles
at the lip, the truth of its color
a very particular sky blue
and no memories of this bowl
in her hand. Yet
I don't leave it in the sink
where the press of plates
could weaken its bonds
and take care that no chipping
pot leans against it because
this was her bowl
and is my morning.

STILL LIFE WITH SANDY

Small photo taped to the wall
the two of us, as we were
denim speckled with blue paint.
Hers the blue eyes and red hair.
She bumps against the picture's cropped edge
as if rising, tired of the wallpaper she's become.

She came to help.
I was painting over old ghosts, fearful
my lover wouldn't live to warm the room.
Behind us, a photograph: Tilden Beach, love-struck
Jackie and I in our "only got eyes for you" newness.
Sandy's hand on that camera. Love can be that rude.
We were friends made of rejected desire.

But in the now of this picture, two friends
are meeting the camera's gaze. We lean forward
into Jackie's last year. She holds the camera.
The camera uses film. Change is in the nature of things.
Sandy was the friend who appeared when needed
and left before the paint dried.

Sandy of Nebraska gave herself the last name
"Seagift." She liked other people's Jewishness
and had the chutzpah to draw mermaids
of herself. When she needed me, I came.
We were friends like that. She tilted towards
her last year, and apologized: need can seem so cruel.
But isn't. But wasn't. I saw the last of her fine red hair
float on a blanket's weave.

Sandy floats to the picture's cropped edge:
Who has taken to bed? Where is the brush?

Lessons from the Greek

I make my entrance
into the compressed pain
of the hospital room:
best friend in the bed, her lover at hand,
attendants in and out, cued by the call light
and choir of infusion pumps beeping
as their numbers land on empty.
Here the discharge planner's unexpected arrival
is expected. Her rudeness a variable.
The repeated pronouncement of imminent eviction,
each time a little louder
—we think she regards our protests a deafness

but she has her own distractions: at night
there is the problem of closed doors
long aisles of them; never a key which fits,
never a hinge or knob. She twists rope into bell
pulls, pounds her fists raw, listens with palms flat
on splintered surfaces; never, not even once,
an answer. By day there is the hospital's
deceptive lack of privacy. She enters doors
already opened, curtains already pulled back.
Her dead son is everywhere
but the room she's in.

Nothing charms her story to a different conclusion.
Consigned to daily rounds, she gives the information
her job demands, then offers the secret handshake:
her son; the name of a protein drink he had liked.
Has she crossed paths with Demeter and Orpheus?
Does she know why, even now, she guards his name?

The monitors blink their solitary eyes.
Let them go dark.
My friend is in the cave
and her name is Nobody.

MAGGIE

Orpheus and I hold guest passes to the underworld;
once in, we do quick work laying words on the missing ground.
Returning—we always return—sometimes we find breadcrumbs,
sometimes salt.

In this story, it is Eurydice who looks back, a shadow
who can't resist the pull of night.

And in this one, it's my first movie with subtitles:
Death dresses as a skeleton and Orfeu sings the sun up.

Also my first encounter with a revolving door
too small to push it, too slow to leap out.

*

No wind. Something else carries his song
to me. We walk on missing ground
credit the dead with our echoing steps.

Bread and salt bless a new home.
We feed the amnesiac dead on blood
hoping to hear our names again.

In this story, Eurydice is the lesson:
to return is to turn back;

Orpheus is the revolving door:
a man of severed head, singing.

*

I hide in his diminishing shadow
press against his calves
his shoulders. Pass through.

Salt raked like sand
an invitation
will she come?

Will she be glad and of company?
How many weeks
to unmake a self?

*

To outrace the speed of light
physicists postulate
a wormhole.

I press into his shadow
and re-enter the darkness
Orpheus lamenting and always

Eurydice turning away.

Blue jays flock to the metaphor of crumbs
and are not fed. Story strips me

like the breath she took and didn't return.

*

Bread and salt; there is no short cut
through decades of talk. Mnemosyne
cannot lead me in or out. I see Maggie

through the moving glass of the theater's door,
give her name to time and get my ticket to its end.

TIMEPIECE

She was the queen of garage sale shopping while I couldn't purchase a pair of socks at Penney's without it turning into a different color and threadbare by the time I got home. Normally I wouldn't enter a narrow shop on an expensive street or peer through a scratched-glass display case at half-hidden wares: but I did. Pocket watches, price tags attached by threads, tiny numbers of incredible length. I kept looking for a decimal point to move the zeros to a more likely column. This watch, the one revealed when I asked if there was anything cheaper. A hundred dollars suddenly seemed a bargain: I ran to the bank and returned and the owner did something which brought the hands to the right time and I said something appropriate to it being a liquidation sale and he said something companionable along the lines of so it goes.

I didn't know what the watch looked like except big and silver. I was afraid to take it out of my pocket because it had cost a hundred dollars and maybe someone would want it for just that reason. I felt foolish for both the fear and the expense but knew I would get used to both. At home, I put it on the dresser. And then the desk. I was getting used to it. I had to see that the needle hands were difficult for me to see. I had to know that silver was not my first choice for anything. And I had to feel how good, how very good it felt in my hand. It filled my palm. I could enclose it within two hands. It did not seem like something easy to lose. It had mass, something gravity could pull on. And I recognized the shape of summer—it was just barely July and I realized that time was larger than minutes and nothing but imagination kept this watch from always being the watch we kept over her.

The watch began to glow with significance. I could look at it and cry. I could hold it and be comforted. I looked forward to the time we would share. But on the evening of the second day the hands stopped moving. I had no receipt. I wondered if I'd been cheated. The watch represented every time I'd been a fool. It was worthless. It was death reduced, a flat stone for skipping across the water. A paperweight. If she were here, she'd have something to tell me about taking things so hard.

BASIC WRITING

A minor bravery of words
taping themselves to the page
thin bodies sticky with effort, letters
crawling up each other's spines, then sprawled
distant as one arc of an *o* from another.
A language called forth by *there's no call for that.*

Nouns will probably get in their way: too many
griefs to startle *cry,* timbre sloughed at the margin line.
Ants might be the better subject: communal
survivors herding aphids into winter burrows
aphids of memory serving a hungry purpose
words like ants surfacing before rain.

THINGS TO CONSIDER

Water in a bucket when the moon is full
knows something of desire and limits

Ink wants a return to wholeness
the sea uncorrupted by distinctions

I can see, between the window's grille, a half-page of ocean
scribbled with thin white lines

The view from the beach is different: the white caps are drowning
they bob briefly to the surface and then go under

WHAT WE KNOW

I think it is the sedative of narcotics
which gives dying people the quiet
to name their dying. When I hold her
neither of us screams
though we are looking death
straight in each other's eye.
Then she blinks,
"What if this treatment doesn't work?"
As if it could. I bite my tongue.
She slurs her words.
I want to shake her back
into the breaking heart
of knowing the story's end
but she knows it.
She is the breaking heart.
And then I am.

NETTLE

Her days are narrow and delicate
as a nettle slid inside skin.
Once she brought her dying cat
to be put down by a vet's needle,
now she reaches for help
without euphemism
a display of pills on the table.
With seemly hesitation
her friends make reply:
a prior experience
a dictionary of pharmaceuticals
abiding love and a bitter ignorance
tasting,
the text suggests,
like drugs in water.

She requests the Shirelles'
Don't Say Goodnight and Mean Goodbye
but nothing sounds ironic
only sweet nostalgia while
in the kitchen a slice and dice
of small hard beads,
an attempt to keep count.

They bring her tea and pudding.
Yellow grains float out of suspension
gather like sugar at the cup's bottom

and must be retrieved.
They spoon liquid
into her mouth
carry bitterness
in chocolate.
More? she asks.
More, they answer.
Two spoons. She turns,
baby bird, towards each.

"Guess I'll never see you two again."
They answer with a blanket of kisses.
Her breaths soften towards sleep then
jerk open
a sonorous rasping.
They sit like angels in a lullaby
quietly attentive
as if they could ride her breath to the inside
and learn something.

They sit.
They sip tea.
They eat cookies.
They sit they get up they sit they stretch they
offer and take or decline. Her breath

becomes gentle as waves

which are endless.
Frightened,
they become stone trying to teach flesh
the way to cease.

The immensity of death is revealed:
a small dark hole, a needle's eye
they can not thread her through.

In the ninth hour they lie down,
ears still leashed to breath
as if by connection
it could be broken.

Her friends wake up.
The sun is shining.
She is still breathing.
Except for the frozen circle
of her mouth,
she looks like herself.
And when
her breath does
finally
stop

even now
they are
listening

BACKLIT

Some people put on the day
one leg at a time
becoming
a person
of habits

even though
their nights
are streaked walls
of headlights
and amputation.

They seem to themselves
all shadow
because the sun
follows at their back;
they believe themselves
invisible
because it hurts us
to look.

KADDISH

The rituals get confused by suicide,
their purpose stumbles between disbelief
and the supermarket shelf: matza ball mix,
Chanukah gelt, candles for the anniversary
of a death, this my Judaica shop,
condensed soup, frozen pizza, a rueful light.
Back home, I light the candle all wrong. Premature.
Yahrzeits are for year's marking. More proper
is a glass with tallow for seven days, if one knew
when to begin. His death hour, undiscovered.
My relationship, unsanctioned: the ex-sister-in-law,
if there'd been wedding or divorce.
David. I cup the light like a Sabbath wife
carry glow between my palms, rinse my face
and dip again. David
who laid himself down as for sleep
whose blanket was paranoia
whose sheets were pain
whose pillow was loneliness and there he wept
whose messages were returned
opened, unopened, read, unread
who fell inside my witness and falls still
I place you on the kitchen counter
beside the dishes and the toaster
your wax smell infusing breakfast,
then move you through the rooms of my day.
Your death makes you light and easier to carry.

ECCLESIASTES

Night comes by dark and by habit, the earth rolling over
the sun turning away, one backward glance gilding the horizon.
The dead swallow their lives whole, in a gulp, like the raw egg
of a hangover remedy. But that's no reason to ignore them
or the returning brilliance of day.

The Parting of Speech

PISTACHIOS

What do I know about us
that is not mundane and incredible?
I see our appetites, our frustrations,
our death, our hope
for someone
(preferably ourselves)
to name how we experienced
(without unique claim to any of it)
salted pistachios:

shells pinching the tongue
the mouth, salt-lined, alerting the brain
to possibilities: sea breeze, seasickness,
the moist remains clinging like a day
at the boardwalk, the end of that day
when to be tired means well-spent
and the body says *no more pistachios*
and *give me more.*

Silence Is a Dragon's Hoard
but words belong to the people

We are
dragonflies and mites
a swarm of no-see-ums composing
love sonnets and jeremiads
—a dime a dozen
and a fiscal fact:
poets pay more than a pretty
penny to approach the gates
of publication, something Marx
or Smith could explain though not
to my satisfaction. Yet
there they are: alphabet coins
jingling in the pocket
magician'd out of the air
stolen from the family vault
sprung free of the spasm'd throat
etched in prison styrofoam
subject to myriad forms
of erasure and available
on every cracked sidewalk
beside the leaves of grass.

AMERICAN LIFE

Everything changes. Everyone says that.
Streets change with the financial pages;
shops beg for rent and people make doorway homes.
Chain stores replace the Mom & Pops, then leave.
We do not have what it takes to keep them.
Only the Caterpillars, the yellow winged bombs,
the bright missiles do not change, and we
cannot keep them here either.

Someone's Work

Into the workday
    let slip the daydream

Into the night dream
    let slip the light of passing cars

Into the cars
    let slip families slapping cards face down
        face up, the game of war

Let fall from wars the families face up face down
    slip on their names, the ones so loose
        so common, anyone could call them home.

KATRINA

Words beat against the pier of an attic wall.

Our names set loose on the water, then stopped
trapped in plaster.

Debris has its own pressing need and rats
their urge to clean our nests.

A foul breath on the water
but it isn't ours.

THIS SPACE RESERVED

the white
margins
are open
wide
for a poet
writing
in a script
I can't
read
of
horrors
I pretend
to imagine.

Afghanistan
Palestine
Somalia
Haiti
my city, east
and west

if I say
more
there
is less.

WHILE EVERYONE ELSE AT THE RALLY
SINGS "AMAZING GRACE"

I am thinking how lucky
not to be born a wretch like thee.

Where I came from *grace* was other girls'
agility and *–less*
the tight hamstrings we sisters shared.

Where we were raised, our sins
were our own; redemption
lay within reach
like the socks left on the floor
to tempt our mother's rage. We were
bad but no one invoked a *thou shalt not.*
Mom didn't need a god for back up.

Human and deity, not child and parent.
He saw and he knew.
One could be embarrassed, even ashamed,
before him. But prayers floated
like wishes on the dandelion's halo.
And when the neighbors' baby died
no one said *we'll understand by and by*
or *punished.*

We cursed our parents' evil ways
as they cursed ours, freely, without belief
in damnation. This was the tree of knowledge
which our parents planted. Watch us turn
crooked cartwheels beneath its branches,
falling gratefully head over heels over head.

Gaylord's Ghazal

Tables for two, groups of five, a book and a bun in the café.
On Friday it seemed everyone knew someone in the café.

The naming of coffee Sunrise, Sumatra, 1816.
Paper napkins, plastic stirrers, yesterday a gun in the café.

A public privacy, a private commons, laptops and wi-fi
amid the clatter, hearts being won in the café.

Ceiling fan, open window: Lotus Thai, Mille Fiori
my words lie flat as acrylics hung in the café.

Cataract of stone to pebble to sand, a lined surface to ink
Tuesday it was Maggie's death I wished undone in the café.

Why the music is older than the clientele I don't know
today I begin with tea and end in a pun at the café.

CAFÉ MUSE

In the corner of every good writer's imagination
a woman sits by a window at a café table
lit by shadow:
she's best when partly revealed.
Her face is lined or unwritten, naïve,
posture indicative of ennui or a wait
limned with subtle anxiety.
Her hand cups a cigarette.
If she holds a book, she soon puts it down
and the manner of its placement—
closed as a dead end
opened so pages turn themselves
—presages the novel's arc.

To feed imagination, these writers
observe strangers in public places.
I have quit smoking; the light is summer soft
early evening; have patience: it is for you
that I am regarding a macchiato
and considering the spoon.

TREADMILL

Striding boldly
and going nowhere
with great satisfaction
because I've mastered—no
because I still can—and quickly
as evidenced by fine line of sweat
upon the brow and the ability to sing
only snatches of "Time Is On My Side"
as I go.

Age Is

Age is a terrible noticing
mainly of self.
At the café
the methodical movement
of salt, pepper and jam
away; the drag of cream, closer;
a settling of book and eyeglasses
perhaps a pen and notebook;
finally the paper napkin.

I watch myself from another table:
why does that woman need things just so?
And argue back, querulous,
I'm not fussy, I just
—Age is noticing stupid recurrent thoughts
without a corresponding memory
of when "making space on a table"
was unremarkable, non-symptomatic.

I imagine it is stiffness settling in,
that premature rigor mortis which
prompts people to buy brain games
and watch, with sidling glance,
for witnesses to pratfall (youth does
a quick slip-fall red-faced recovery;
age slides on the peel a full two stanzas
then lands   on the caesura).

WAITING

Against the walls of her good fortune
a woman sits in her aging. The chairs
are green. First floor is mail boxes,
guest sign-in, hairdresser, rattan. Third,
medical station, more apartments, her home
on the far coast of her children's lives.
Stride to stumble, walker to attendant,
the possibilities move past her on their way to lunch.
If death does not find them here, there are other destinations:
the home for the further aged or the fourth floor.

The fourth floor has an aquarium, a beautiful tank,
a yard or more of glass. Once she dragged the family up
to view mollies, oscars and koi.
She was always like that: owning things,
understanding these fish as part of her landscape
while her children blushed, embarrassed intruders
on the dementia unit. "Buzz in, buzz out,"
she nodded, indicating the locked door. Two years later
she keeps on the right side of it though words slip
past the hook of speech. She calls after them
casting abracadabra into the pool where it falls,
sinks. She names the ripple, "Isn't it awful?"

It will be awful but now the brain is caught in a mirror
twisting, trying to catch the reflection of knowledge:
I gave the children my checkbook, there's a time for everything,
but falling? Would I forget falling? Three times
fifty is still a solid number. I told them I should make a will—
why would I say that when I know my mind is labeled in a folder?
Dinner starts at five; movie at seven. Thursday is fish
floating colors on a paper wall.

APPLE PIE

This apple pie would never fool anyone
who had eaten apple pie. It fools the one
who needs apple pie and has not the
wherewithal, has never learned to pare
the apple to roll the crust to time the oven
to find a bakery and therefore is the one who
buys pie from a row of plastic-sealed cousins
cherry, peach, blueberry, chooses apple because
she did know what it could taste like though she
also knows from experience that it will not. This
is a pie she has had before with the same tea
which at least tastes like tea and rinses the
disappointment out of her day.

The Metaphor

and I shall sail away in my grammar boat, telling the students: Look. See. I have drawn a half circle representing the body of a boat and a line perpendicular to its diameter — notice please the relevance of geometry—*verb* is the boat, *subject* the captain on its deck, sail unfurls on the perpendicular if our sentence has a *complete thought*. I sail away so pleased with that image and hope you are too; some will despair over mastering a reverberation with so few echoes and a chili bowl on the board with a spoon handle sticking out of it which is wrong: it is a boat now swiftly encumbered, an adverb clinging to its side, and a balloon of description floating above the captain.

Sentences float on water, but essays travel asphalt. They are buses, or bus routes, no, buses. As follows: *introduction* names the bus we're getting on—it's the sign above the window behind which we readers spy you in the driver's seat not unlike the captain on a boat's deck only you are not the essay's subject except who can escape the ego and the first assignment, "A Learning Experience." Now we're on the bus making stops at all those lovely paragraphs, grateful for the *topic sentence* street signs—have I mentioned boxes yet? *paragraphs* are packing boxes: imagine you are packing your ideas for a move—clothes in one box, kitchen supplies in another, a label on each carton so you—well don't worry

about that now because what you need to know for
tomorrow's test is how your teacher sails away on a Mary
Poppins umbrella where the fabric is your *topic* and the ribs
—yes, our ribs, spare ribs, Adam's rib, umbrella... spokes? not
ribs? both right? the ribs are sentences supporting the topic
and the handle the *thesis* to which they all connect. Rest while

I sail away who only once stood on a deck: Long Island
Sound and doesn't that take one away not as subtraction but
a memory of nasal voices, city migrants so surprised to be in
water water everywhere and slightly mal de mer. This is how
I am sailing away: without nautical knowledge. This is how I
will sail away: as if there were a shore I left called Reason
where metaphors are collective and useful in the way that
the image of a sun god in his chariot illuminates the passage
of a day, the way we say "sunset years" and "sundowning"—
will you think you see me sailing away when I strap boxes of
metaphor to my feet and skate out on the water like an insect
whose name I've forgotten or never known, forgetful if my
errand is eating or being eaten? When the sail unfurls at
random, when the captain is a noun substituting for a noun
shouting "Topic!" "Tactic!" "Titanic!" will you mistake this
for "I have no tactic for discussing a topic: help!" while an
imposter shapes my lips for a long island sound? When you
see this body sailing past without a tense, when the bus
never reaches conclusion, trust the handbook's future past
perfect: we will have never been introduced.

NOTES FOR THE PARTING OF SPEECH

When the sun begins its climb
a verb provides the traction.
When feathered waves are singed by light
it's a state of being only verbs can create.
Yet they vex us; they shift endings;
we say verb and tense.

*

Phoebus descending, the golden chariot a rumor
of stars drawn by swans—*of, by*
a glory of prepositions taking on their task,
little tugboats pulling person, place, thing, idea,
the concrete, the abstract, the noun
into relationship with the sentence.
It gives one pause. It makes one think:
useful, yes; how did we join [without] them?

*

Adverbs seem like sensible folk:
they want the story ma'am, the how and when,
the intensity, the frequency, the place. It happened here.
It happened here yesterday and again tomorrow.
Slowly and then not so slowly. They are surprisingly
non-monogamous, attaching themselves with abandon
to verbs, adjectives, and even others of their own kind.
Just for sport, they make noun-struck modifiers
quiver all over.

*

Psyche, mistrustful, goes searching for love
in her lover's face, as if their nightly joinings
are counterfeit, and love a guise of love
a substitution, a pronoun. The story faults
jealous sisters but it is language that does us in.
Eros is an it. Cupid a he. Psyche a she. But we
are love.

*

Nouns, noun complements, adjective nouns,
verbals behaving as nouns, misspellings of
noun—no wonder the sun falls at the coming of night,
each has but one syllable for lifting an enormity
of associations. Object nouns, proper nouns. Gaia
born of Chaos, mother of sea and sky, must fight
her own gravity, bench-pressing sun and night
to open a little space for us, our lumbering nouns,
our noisy litany of gods and laurels, sunlight caught
on the tree line. Small wonder we interject
deleted expletives.

*

The sun continues to orbit the earth.
After all we've been told to the contrary.
Sentences lean towards meaning.
A hive of conjunctions, a Greek chorus
buzzing with rationales: *because, since, so.*
Helpless, we fly.

THE READER

I had, as a child, the nasty habit of eating words right off the page: whole rows of letters—even the angel-tipped serifs— nibbled; the tiny curl ends of j and y, which gathered like toast crumbs in the bindings, licked clean. My gaze would fall on any phrase and falling—instinctively—grab hold; holding naturally turned to tasting, tasting to chewing and so forth. It seemed harmless enough. I was a child. Yet knowing how memory serves its master, maybe I was rough or rude? Why else would my sisters run to our mother complaining that I'd erased their books again? Perhaps I gobbled and gulped and wore the stains of gluttony on my face; where I'd see myself a myopic visionary with the appetite of an escape artist, they'd remember a greedy know-it-all who grabbed their wishes before they could know them.

Truly mine was an indiscriminate hunger—the ubiquitous cereal boxes, my mother's novels—but the books my sisters chose, or had assigned to them, did seem particularly... available. I got there first, cracking spines like wishbones, leaving pages splotched with grease, turning them opaque, translucent when held to the light: they could have seen what remains after reading, but I didn't have the words to tell them.

Psalm for My Parents

I praise the work of their hands
the yes of their daily rising
the man to his labors, the woman to hers.
I praise the instant coffee and the jellied toast
the goldfish crackers and the radio songs
which took him to work and brought him home.
I praise his car. I praise her car

her going in and her going out,
the food purchased and the meals prepared
the wash, the wash, the wash
the insistence on milk at three o'clock
and the books that led us away.

Notes on Greek mythology and Homer's The Odyssey

"Lessons from the Greek"

Demeter, a goddess, searches for her daughter; Orpheus (Orfeu), a musician and poet, searches for his beloved Eurydice; each can be found in Hades, the realm of death.

Captured by the one-eyed Polyphemus, Odysseus (hero of The Odyssey) tells the cyclops that his name is "Nobody"—this, plus poking out his eye, enables Odysseus to avoid death.

"Maggie"

According to the Greeks, Orpheus failed to retrieve Eurydice because he looked back before leading her fully into the land of the living. My poem suggests otherwise.

Mnemosyne is a goddess of memory, mother of the muses, and, in some versions, thereby related to Orpheus.

"Notes for the Parting of Speech"

Indebted to the Greeks for their gods—and East Hills Elementary School where I first made their acquaintance.

Acknowledgements

"1985" earlier version appeared in *Sinister Wisdom: A Journal for the Lesbian Imagination in the Arts and Politics*.

"Ecclesiastes" and "Kaddish" appeared in *Bridges: A Jewish Feminist Journal*.

"How Memory Returns," "On Seeing My Mother" and "Waking" appeared in *Margie: the American Journal of Poetry*.

"Nettle" earlier versions appeared in *Sinister Wisdom* and *Harrington Lesbian Fiction Quarterly*.

"The Reader" and "Still Life with Sandy" appeared in *The Comstock Review*.

With Thanks to the Many

including writing group cohorts, Flight of the Mind, the Mills faculty and MFA class of 2003, with special gratitude to Chana Bloch, and to the students and colleagues at the College of Alameda whose tenacity encourages my own,

including the Bay Area lesbian community which supports its cultural workers, with special thanks to Elana Dykewomon,

including Robin Deeming, Laura Munter, and Gail Stewart for the witnessing,

including Chana Wilson, Helen Mayer and Susan Shulman for a hundred-and-then-some Sundays of conversation, critique and patient revisiting of comma placement. These poems in both craft and heart owe much to their care,

including Susan Liroff for sharing her art and her craft, generously and skillfully translating the manuscript into printed form, and adding her visuals to my voice,

including Richard Lipperman, T. Asher Adar Schaffer and Çagla Ozcan, whose presence can be felt in the space between words,

and in memory of Jackie Winnow, Joanne Garrett, Sandy Seagift, and Maggie Rochlin.